ULTIMATE SCIENCE

PHYSICAL SCIENCE

Elements

Charlotte Deschermeier

Published in 2014 by The Rosen Publishing Group, Inc.
29 East 21st Street, New York, NY 1001 0

Photo Credits: © 2003-2013 Shutterstock, Inc.; p. 7, 9 Wikipedia

Library of Congress Cataloging-in-Publication Data

Deschermeier, Charlotte, author.
Elements / by Charlotte Deschermeier.
pages cm. – (Ultimate science. Physical science)
Includes index.
ISBN 978-1-4777-6085-7 (library) – ISBN 978-1-4777-6086-4 (pbk.) –
ISBN 978-1-4777-6087-1 (6-pack)
1. Periodic table–Juvenile literature. 2. Chemical elements–Juvenile literature. I. Title.
QD467.D47 2014
546–dc23

2013023463

Manufactured in the United States of America

CPSIA Compliance Information: Batch #W14PK4: For Further Information contact Rosen Publishing, New York, New York at 1-800-237-9932

Contents

Elements 4

The History of the Periodic Table 6

Numbers and Symbols 8

Groups and Periods 10

Metals 12

Nonmetals 14

Semiconductors 16

How to Use the Periodic Table 18

Different Kinds of Periodic Tables 20

The Periodic Table of Tomorrow 22

Glossary 23

Index 24

Websites 24

Elements

Atoms make up everything in the world. Things that are made of just one kind of atom are elements. For example, gold is an element. A solid gold coin is made only of gold atoms. There are more than 90 natural elements. Scientists have created over 20 more elements in their labs. Some common natural elements are **oxygen**, iron, and silver. Elements can be solids, liquids, or gases. Most elements are solids at room **temperature.** Every element has its own properties. How an element feels, looks, smells, or acts are some of its properties.

This solid gold coin comes from Japan. All its atoms are gold atoms.

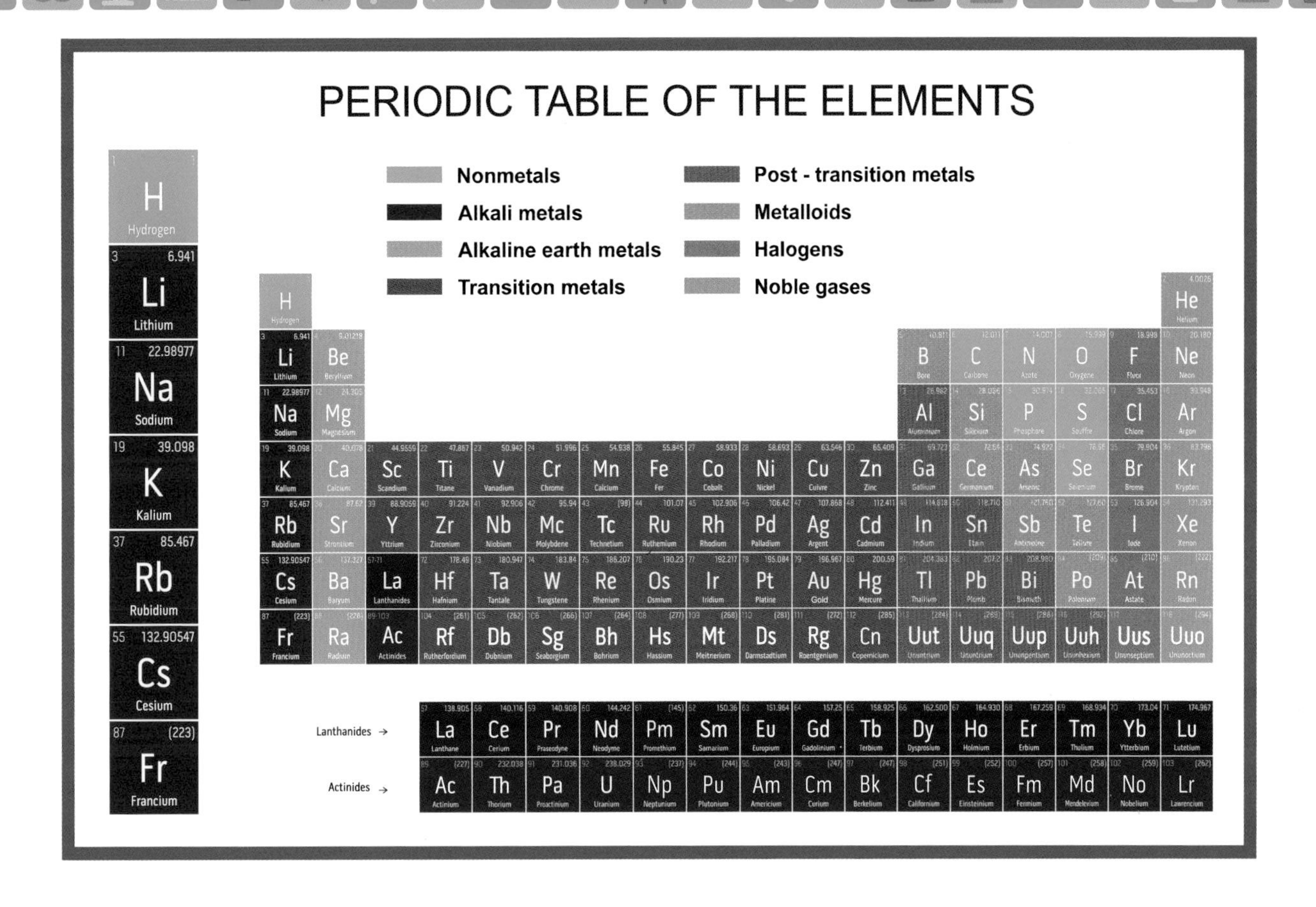

Other properties of elements, such as **mass** and **density,** are also studied by scientists. You can recognize an element by observing its properties. Similarly, if you baked cookies, by observing a cookie's properties, such as its appearance, smell, and taste, your friends would know what kind of cookie you made.

All the 118 known elements are shown on the periodic table (above).

The History of the Periodic Table

Throughout history, people have studied elements. Nine elements were discovered before AD 1. By the 1860s, 63 elements had been found, and scientists needed a good way to keep track of them.

A Russian scientist named Dmitry Mendeleyev wanted to arrange the elements in a chart. Mendeleyev wrote the name of each element on a card. Just as a baseball card has facts about one player, Mendeleyev listed facts about one element on each card. He rearranged the cards and put elements with similar properties together.

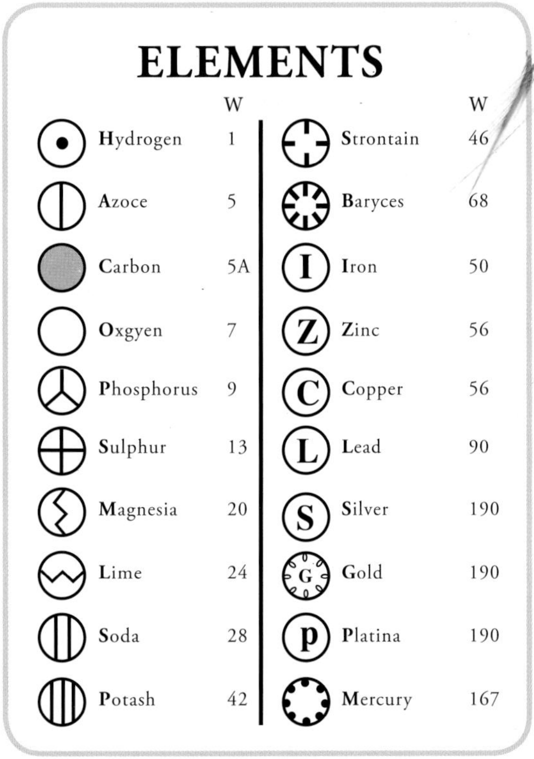

ELEMENTS

Element	W	Element	W
Hydrogen	1	Strontain	46
Azoce	5	Baryces	68
Carbon	5A	Iron	50
Oxgyen	7	Zinc	56
Phosphorus	9	Copper	56
Sulphur	13	Lead	90
Magnesia	20	Silver	190
Lime	24	Gold	190
Soda	28	Platina	190
Potash	42	Mercury	167

In 1808, scientist John Dalton listed the 20 known elements in the chart above.

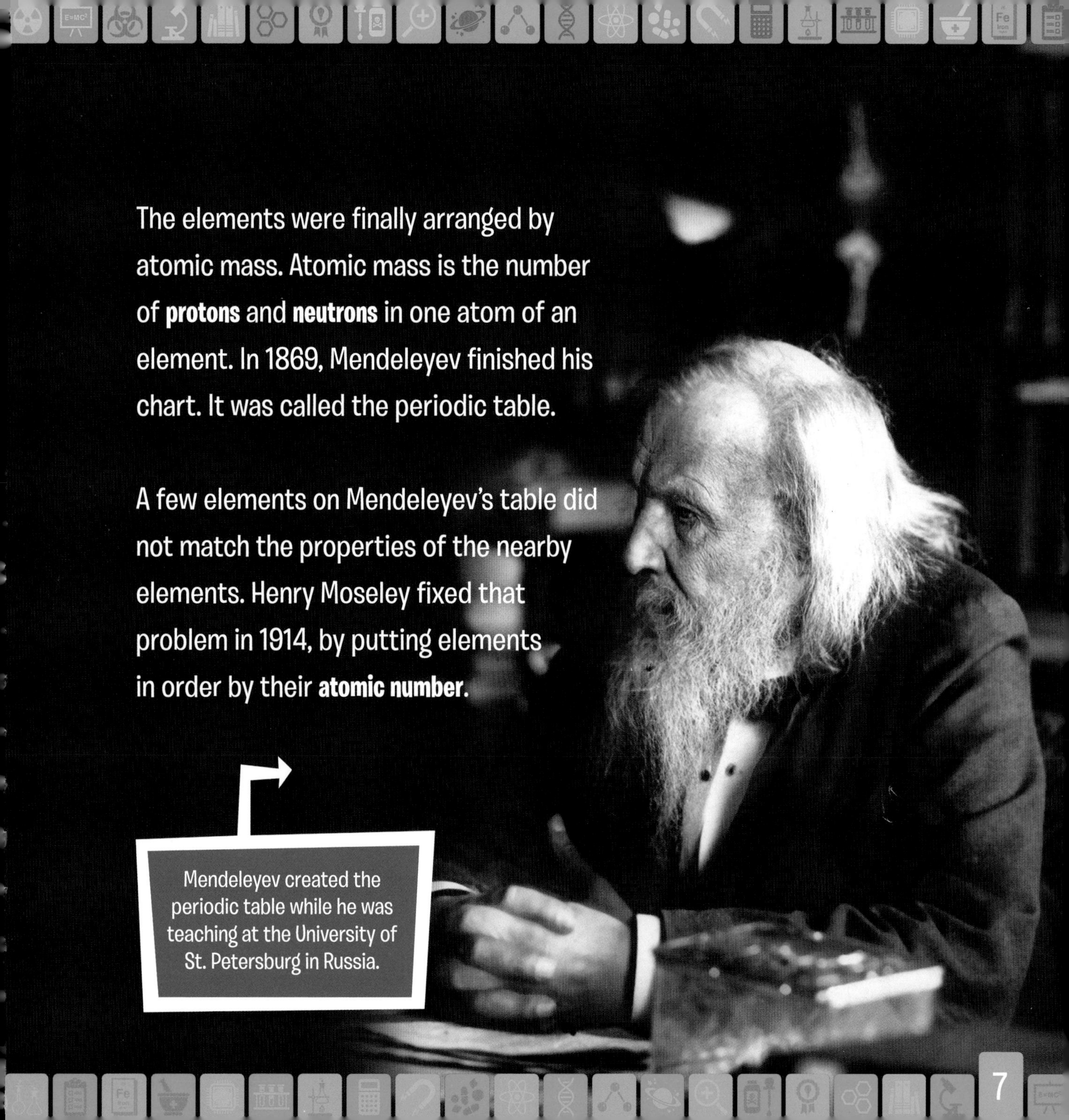

The elements were finally arranged by atomic mass. Atomic mass is the number of **protons** and **neutrons** in one atom of an element. In 1869, Mendeleyev finished his chart. It was called the periodic table.

A few elements on Mendeleyev's table did not match the properties of the nearby elements. Henry Moseley fixed that problem in 1914, by putting elements in order by their **atomic number**.

Mendeleyev created the periodic table while he was teaching at the University of St. Petersburg in Russia.

Numbers and Symbols

The facts about each element is given in one square on the periodic table. For example, the first element on the periodic table is **hydrogen.** Hydrogen's square is green, which means hydrogen is a nonmetal.

Elements are arranged on the periodic table in order of their atomic numbers. An element's atomic number is the number of protons in one atom of that element. For example, hydrogen's atomic number is one because it has one proton.

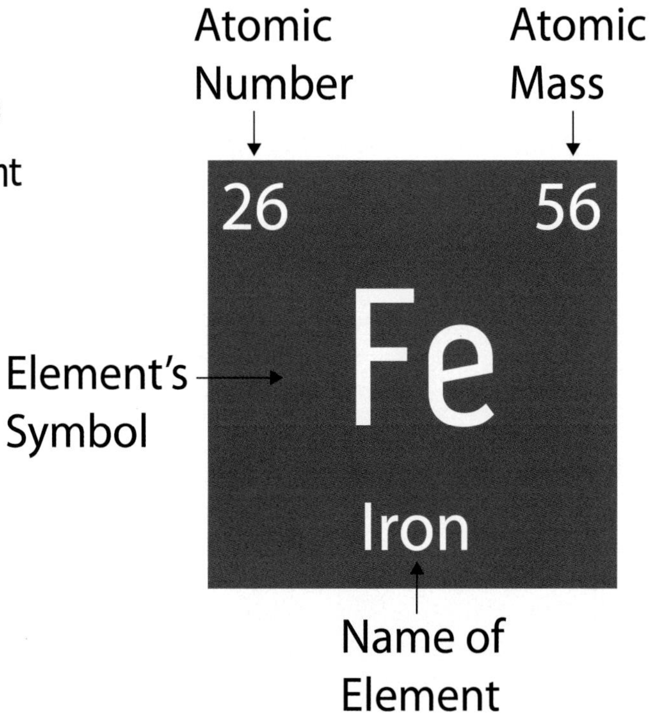

Atomic Number
Atomic Mass
26
56
Element's Symbol
Fe
Iron
Name of Element

An element's name is written below its symbol. The atomic mass is in the top right corner of that element's square.

At the top left corner of the element's square is the atomic number. In the center of each square is a one-, two-, or three-letter **symbol** for the element. Sometimes the symbol is the first letter of the element's name, like H for hydrogen. Some symbols come from the name of the element in another language. The Latin word for "iron" is *ferrum*. Iron's symbol is Fe. Some elements are named after famous scientists. Einsteinium is named after Albert Einstein. Es is its symbol.

Albert Einstein lived from 1879 to 1955. He made many important scientific discoveries.

Groups and Periods

A group is a **column** on the periodic table. There are 18 groups of elements, and each is named by its column number. Some groups have all metal elements, and some have only gas elements. Other groups are a mix of different kinds of elements.

Elements in each group have similar properties. This means they look or act alike under certain conditions. For example, the elements found in Group 18 are gases. These gases have no color, odor, or taste. This group has been called the noble gases.

Group 1 of the periodic table includes the alkali metals. Lithium is an alkali metal used in making batteries.

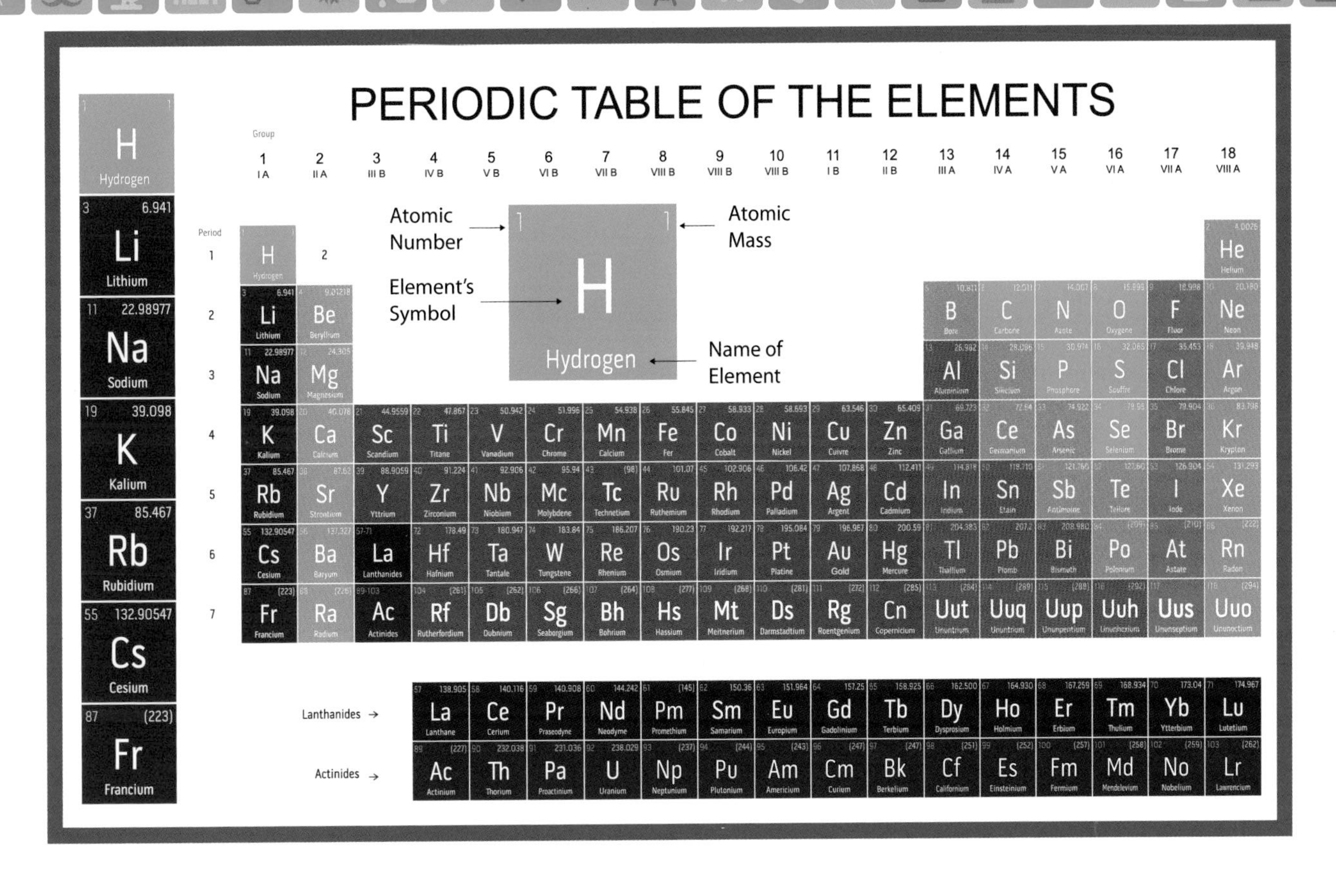

Periods are the rows of elements. They are called periods because properties of elements are periodic as you move across the row. This means they show up again. Below the periodic table, a part of periods six and seven are shown, so that the entire table can fit on a page.

Except for hydrogen, all the elements in the first group of the periodic table are alkali metals.

Metals

There are three large groups that the elements in the periodic table have been divided into. These groups are metals, nonmetals, and semiconductors. Most of the elements are metals. They are found in the middle of and to the left of the periodic table.

Of the 118 elements in the periodic table, 91 are metals.

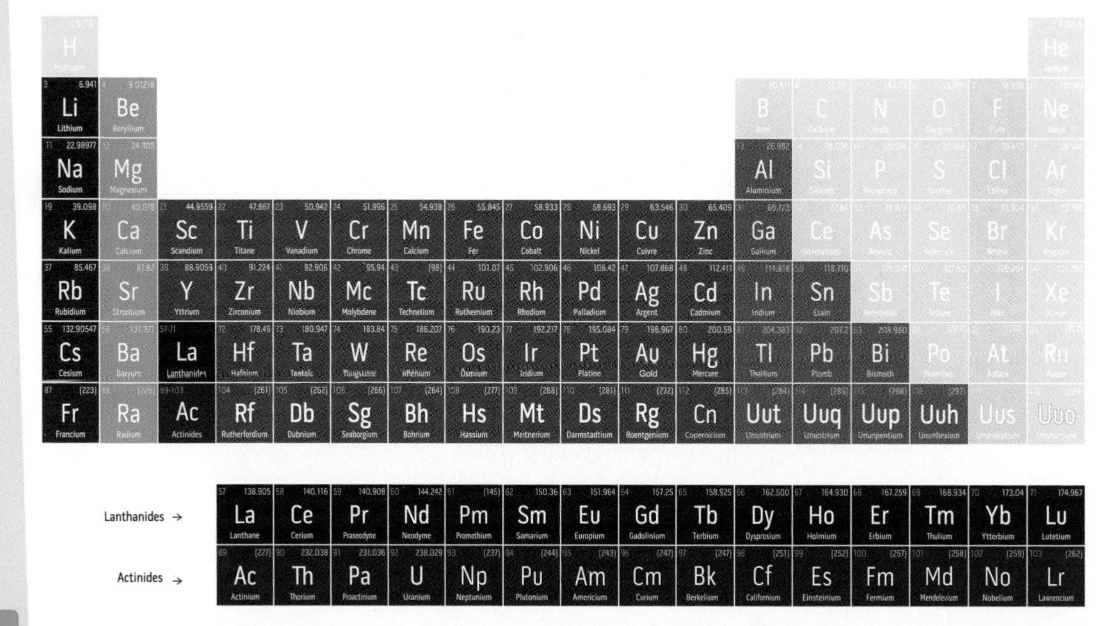

The properties of metals make them useful. Many metals are strong. These metals are used to make buildings, bridges, and tools. Coins are also made of metal. Metal can carry electricity. Electric wires are made of metal. Most metals conduct heat. That is why baking and cooking pans are made of metal. Some metals, like aluminum, can be flattened into thin sheets. Sheets of aluminum are used to make cans for food. Pressed even thinner, aluminum becomes foil. Shiny metals, such as gold and silver, are made into rings and necklaces. A thin piece of silver is placed behind glass to make a **mirror**. A world without metal is hard to imagine.

Metals work well for building bridges, because they are both strong and easy to shape.

Nonmetals

Nonmetals are the second-largest group of elements. More than half the nonmetals are gases. All nonmetals are on the right side of the periodic table, except for hydrogen. Hydrogen is at the top left corner of the table because its atomic number is one. However, it has properties like those of other nonmetals.

The word "nonmetals" means "not like metals." Nonmetals have many properties that are the opposite of the properties of metals. For example, solid nonmetals are not shiny. The nonmetal sulfur has a dull surface. Unlike metals, nonmetals cannot be flattened into other shapes.

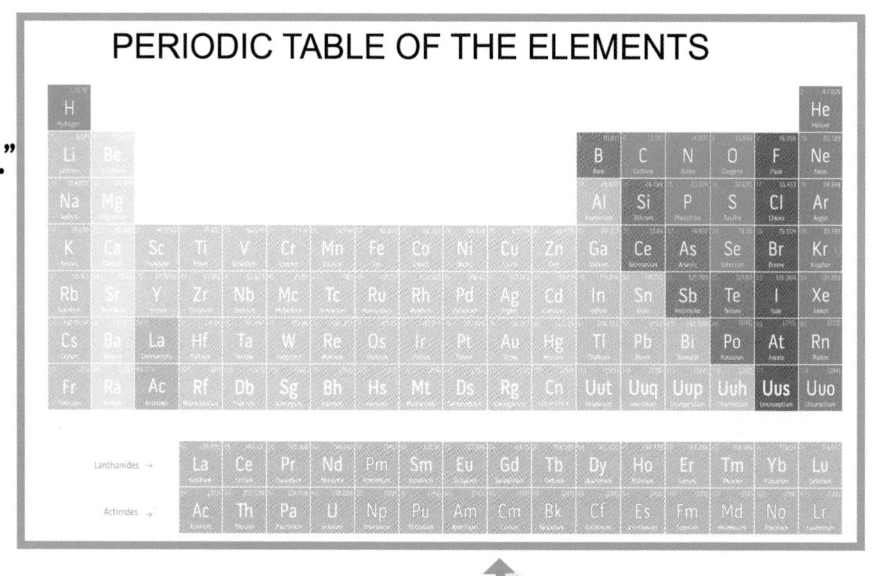

Hydrogen is in the periodic table's top left corner. The rest of the nonmetals are on the right.

In pencil lead, you find the nonmetal carbon. If you press hard on your pencil, the tip will break, not bend. Nonmetals do not conduct heat or electricity as well as metals do.

Nonmetal elements are important to living things. More than 95 percent of your body is made of the nonmetals oxygen, carbon, hydrogen, and **nitrogen.** Mostly nonmetals make up people, animals, and plants.

This man is mining sulfur in Indonesia. People use sulfur to make plants grow better and to bleach, or whiten, things.

Semiconductors

There are very few semiconductors. Semiconductors earned their name because they conduct a small amount of electricity. Semiconductors are also called metalloids. They are located on a zigzag line between the metals and the nonmetals on the periodic table.

Semiconductors are above the metals and below the nonmetals on the periodic table.

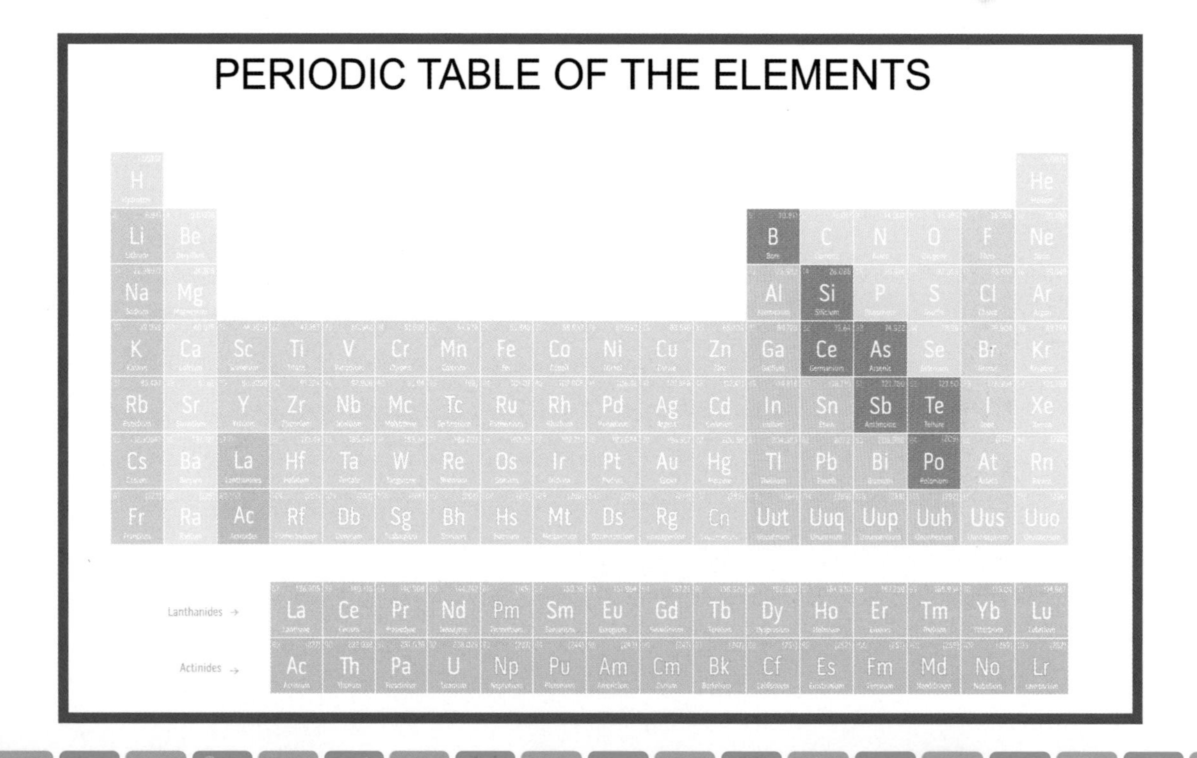

Semiconductors share some properties with metals as well as nonmetals. For example, tellurium looks like a shiny metal, but it also breaks as easily as a nonmetal does. Another semiconductor called boron is very hard but breaks easily. It can conduct electricity only when it is heated to a high temperature.

The chips above are made from the semiconductor silicon. Silicon chips are used in computers, radios, and cell phones.

Silicon has become an important and well-known semiconductor. It is used to make tiny chips that are found in computers, video games, and digital cameras. Silicon is also used to make special glue for showers, windows, and doors.

How to Use the Periodic Table

At first glance, the periodic table may resemble a large board game that you do not know how to play. But, if you take a closer look, you will find that it is easy to use and find out facts about elements using the periodic table.

Many students use the periodic table in their science classes.

Groups of elements share like properties, so an element's position on the table helps you know its properties. For example, suppose your science teacher asks you to tell the class about the element krypton. You can use the periodic table to get facts about krypton quickly. When you find krypton, you will see that it is on the right side of the table. Immediately you know it is a nonmetal. Then you will see that the other elements in krypton's group are gases, so you can guess that krypton is a gas, too. Inside krypton's square you will find its atomic number, mass, and symbol. You can tell a lot about an element from the information in the periodic table!

These lightbulbs have krypton inside them. Krypton lightbulbs make a bright, white light.

Different Kinds of Periodic Tables

There is more than one form for the periodic table. Hundreds of different periodic tables are used today. These tables were created because different people need different facts about elements. For example, a young student who is just learning about the elements might use a table that shows only whether elements are solids, liquids, or gases. A table for a high-school student might provide the names and the properties of each group of elements. A scientist might need a table that shows how the **electrons** are arranged in the atoms of an element.

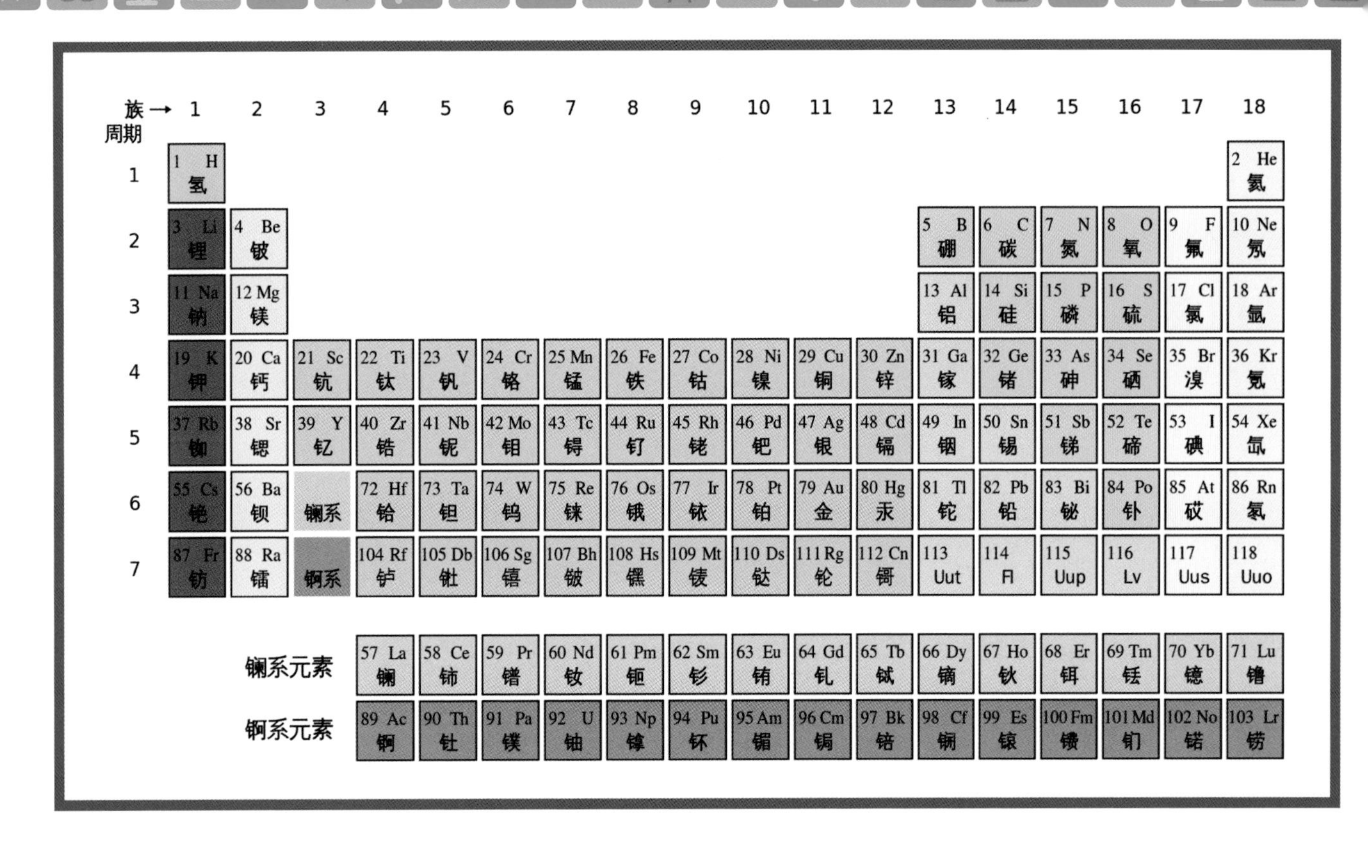

族 → 周期	1	2	3	4	5	6	7	8	9	10	11	12	13	14	15	16	17	18
1	1 H 氢																	2 He 氦
2	3 Li 锂	4 Be 铍											5 B 硼	6 C 碳	7 N 氮	8 O 氧	9 F 氟	10 Ne 氖
3	11 Na 钠	12 Mg 镁											13 Al 铝	14 Si 硅	15 P 磷	16 S 硫	17 Cl 氯	18 Ar 氩
4	19 K 钾	20 Ca 钙	21 Sc 钪	22 Ti 钛	23 V 钒	24 Cr 铬	25 Mn 锰	26 Fe 铁	27 Co 钴	28 Ni 镍	29 Cu 铜	30 Zn 锌	31 Ga 镓	32 Ge 锗	33 As 砷	34 Se 硒	35 Br 溴	36 Kr 氪
5	37 Rb 铷	38 Sr 锶	39 Y 钇	40 Zr 锆	41 Nb 铌	42 Mo 钼	43 Tc 锝	44 Ru 钌	45 Rh 铑	46 Pd 钯	47 Ag 银	48 Cd 镉	49 In 铟	50 Sn 锡	51 Sb 锑	52 Te 碲	53 I 碘	54 Xe 氙
6	55 Cs 铯	56 Ba 钡	镧系	72 Hf 铪	73 Ta 钽	74 W 钨	75 Re 铼	76 Os 锇	77 Ir 铱	78 Pt 铂	79 Au 金	80 Hg 汞	81 Tl 铊	82 Pb 铅	83 Bi 铋	84 Po 钋	85 At 砹	86 Rn 氡
7	87 Fr 钫	88 Ra 镭	锕系	104 Rf 𬬻	105 Db 𬭊	106 Sg 𬭳	107 Bh 𬭛	108 Hs 𬭶	109 Mt 鿏	110 Ds 𫟼	111 Rg 𬬭	112 Cn 鿔	113 Uut	114 Fl	115 Uup	116 Lv	117 Uus	118 Uuo
镧系元素				57 La 镧	58 Ce 铈	59 Pr 镨	60 Nd 钕	61 Pm 钷	62 Sm 钐	63 Eu 铕	64 Gd 钆	65 Tb 铽	66 Dy 镝	67 Ho 钬	68 Er 铒	69 Tm 铥	70 Yb 镱	71 Lu 镥
锕系元素				89 Ac 锕	90 Th 钍	91 Pa 镤	92 U 铀	93 Np 镎	94 Pu 钚	95 Am 镅	96 Cm 锔	97 Bk 锫	98 Cf 锎	99 Es 锿	100 Fm 镄	101 Md 钔	102 No 锘	103 Lr 铹

The periodic tables used in other countries look different from the ones we use in the United States. For example, in China, on a periodic table, the names of the elements are written with Chinese characters along with the letter symbols. Though this periodic table may look different, it still provides useful facts about the elements.

This periodic table uses Chinese characters to list the names of the elements.

The Periodic Table of Tomorrow

The periodic table is constantly undergoing changes by scientists to include new elements. When a new element is created, it is given a name that comes from its atomic number until a final name is chosen. When scientists created an element with 112 protons in 1996, they named it ununbium. This name comes from the Latin words for the numbers in 112. In 2010, the official name of ununbium was changed to copernicium.

Elements have been named after states, countries, and scientists. There is even an element named after a school. In 1950, scientists at the University of California at Berkeley created an element with 97 protons. They named the element berkelium for their school. Scientists continue to make more elements, and the periodic table continues to grow.

Glossary

atomic number (uh-TAH-mik NUM-ber) The number of protons in the center of an atom.

atoms (A-temz) The smallest parts of elements that can exist either alone or with other elements.

column (KAH-lum) A row that goes up and down.

density (DEN-seh-tee) The heaviness of an object compared to its size.

electrons (ih-LEK-tronz) Small parts of an atom that spin around its center.

hydrogen (HY-dreh-jen) A colorless gas that burns easily and weighs less than any other known element.

mass (MAS) The amount of matter in something.

mirror (MIR-ur) A flat surface that shows an exact picture of something placed in front of it.

neutrons (NOO-tronz) Small parts of an atom with a neutral electric charge.

nitrogen (NY-truh-jen) A gas without taste, color, or odor that can be found in the air.

oxygen (OK-sih-jen) A gas that has no color, taste, or odor and is necessary for people and animals to breathe.

protons (PROH-tonz) Small parts of an atom with a positive electric charge.

symbol (SIM-bul) The letter or letters that stand for an element.

temperature (TEM-pur-cher) How hot or cold something is.

Index

A
atomic number(s), 7-9, 14, 19, 22
atom(s), 4, 7-8, 20

D
density, 5

E
Einstein, Albert, 9

G
gas(es), 4, 10, 14, 19-20
group(s), 10, 12, 14, 19-20

H
hydrogen, 8-9, 14-15

L
liquids, 4, 20

M
mass, 5, 19
metal(s), 10, 12-17

N
nonmetal(s), 8, 12, 14-17, 19

O
oxygen, 4, 15

P
properties, 4-7, 10-11, 13-14, 17, 19-20

S
semiconductors, 16-17
solids, 4, 20

Websites

Due to the changing nature of Internet links, PowerKids Press has developed an online list of websites related to the subject of this book. This site is updated regularly. Please use this link to access the list:
www.powerkidslinks.com/usps/elemen/